5/22

SMART MONEY CHOICES

by Jennifer Boothroyd

Consultant: Beth Gambro
Reading Specialist, Yorkville, Illinois

BEARPORT
PUBLISHING

Minneapolis, Minnesota

Teaching Tips

Before Reading

- Look at the cover of the book. Discuss the picture and the title.

- Ask readers to brainstorm a list of what they already know about how they can be smart with their money. What can they expect to see in the book?

- Go on a picture walk, looking through the pictures to discuss vocabulary and make predictions about the text.

During Reading

- Read for purpose. Encourage readers to think about the role money plays in their lives as they are reading.

- Ask readers to look for the details of the book. What are they learning about making smart money choices?

- If readers encounter an unknown word, ask them to look at the sounds in the word. Then, ask them to look at the rest of the page. Are there any clues to help them understand?

After Reading

- Encourage readers to pick a buddy and reread the book together.

- Ask readers to name two ways from the book that they can be smart with money. Go back and find the pages that tell about these things.

- Ask readers to write or draw something they learned about being smart with money.

Credits:
Cover and Title page, © Mtsaride/Shutterstock, © Africa Studio/Shutterstock, and © Trifonov_Evgeniy/iStock; 3, © Ilin Sergey/Shutterstock; 5, © SDI Productions/iStock; 7, © Didecs/Shutterstock, © Pachai Leknettip/Shutterstock; 8–9, © Prostock-studio/Shutterstock; 10, © Chris Ryan/iStock; 12–13, © Group4 Studio/iStock; 14, © Dakalova Iuliia Shutterstock/iStock; 15, © PeopleImages/iStock; 16–17, © andresr/iStock; 18–19, © Deepak Sethi/iStock; 21, © Prostock-Studio/iStock; 22, © New Africa/Shutterstock, © PeopleImages/iStock, © Gelpi/Shutterstock; 23, © bullet74/Shutterstock, © Odua Images/Shutterstock, © Rido/Shutterstock, © ESB Professional/Shutterstock, © ArtSvetlana/Shutterstock

Library of Congress Cataloging-in-Publication Data

Names: Boothroyd, Jennifer, 1972- author.
Title: Smart money choices / by Jennifer Boothroyd.
Description: Minneapolis, MN : Bearport Publishing Company, [2022] |
   Series: Show me the money | Includes bibliographical references and
   index.
Identifiers: LCCN 2021007354 (print) | LCCN 2021007355 (ebook) | ISBN
   9781647479046 (library binding) | ISBN 9781647479114 (paperback) | ISBN
   9781647479183 (ebook)
Subjects: LCSH: Finance, Personal--Juvenile literature. | Money--Juvenile
   literature.
Classification: LCC HG179 .B58425 2022 (print) | LCC HG179 (ebook) | DDC
   332.024--dc23
LC record available at https://lccn.loc.gov/2021007354
LC ebook record available at https://lccn.loc .gov/2021007355

For more information, write to Bearport Publishing, 5357 Penn Avenue South, Minneapolis, MN 55419. Printed in the United States of America.

Contents

Money Wise 4

Money Matters: Keeping Track 22

Glossary 23

Index 24

Read More 24

Learn More Online. 24

About the Author 24

Money Wise

You just got money for your birthday.

Now you have **choices** to make.

What will you do with it?

4

There are many things you can do with money.

You can **save** it.

Or you can give it away.

Maybe you want to **spend** it.

SAVE GIVE SPEND

Saving money means you do not use it right away.

It can be smart to save.

Then, you can buy something big later.

You can give money to someone else.

Some people do not have much.

They may need help.

Giving when you have **extra** is kind.

Another thing to do is spend money.

You can buy things.

Or you can spend money to do things.

Spending means making more big choices.

Before you spend, think about wants and **needs**.

You may want a toy.

But you need a clean toothbrush.

Be smart.

Spend your money on needs first.

Then, think about what to do next.

Maybe you can get something you want.

You can even do it all.

Save some money and give some away.

Spend some on needs and some on wants.

There are so many choices.

Being smart can help you a lot when it comes to money.

Money Matters
Keeping Track

Keep track of how you use money. Get help to write down every time you spend, give, or save.

Take time to look back at what you did. Are you saving, giving, or spending most? What are you spending your money on?

Think about what you learned. Are you making smart choices?

Glossary

choices things that you can pick

extra more than you need

needs things you must have

save to keep something to use later

spend to use money to pay for something

Index

buy 9, 12
choices 4, 12, 20, 22
give 6, 11, 18, 22
needs 14, 16, 18

save 6, 9, 18, 22
spend 6, 12, 14, 16, 18, 22
wants 14, 18

Read More

Higgins, Nadia. *Using Money (Money Smarts).* Minneapolis: Jump!, 2018.

Lindeen, Mary. *Needs and Wants (A Beginning-to-Read Book).* Chicago: Norwood House Press, 2020.

Learn More Online

1. Go to **www.factsurfer.com**
2. Enter "**Smart Money**" into the search box.
3. Click on the cover of this book to see a list of websites.

About the Author

Jenny Boothroyd likes to spend money on fresh fruits and gifts for her family.